This marriage study series is pure Focus on the Family—
reliable, biblically sound and dedicated to reestablishing family values
in today's society. This series will no doubt help a multitude of couples
strengthen their relationship, not only with each other,
but also with God, the *creator* of marriage itself.

Bruce Wilkinson

Author, The BreakThrough Series: *The Prayer of Jabez,*
Secrets of the Vine and *A Life God Rewards*

In this era of such need, Dr. Dobson's team has produced solid,
helpful materials about Christian marriage. Even if they have been
through marriage studies before, every couple—married or engaged—
will benefit from this foundational study of life together. Thanks to
Focus on the Family for helping set us straight in this top priority.

Charles W. Colson

Chairman, Prison Fellowship Ministries

In my 31 years as a pastor, I've officiated at hundreds of weddings.
Unfortunately, many of those unions failed. I only wish the *Focus on the*
Family Marriage Series had been available to me during those years.
What a marvelous tool you as pastors and Christian leaders have
at your disposal. I encourage you to use it to assist those you
serve in building successful, healthy marriages.

H. B. London, Jr.

Vice President, Ministry Outreach/Pastoral Ministries
Focus on the Family

Looking for a prescription for a better marriage?
You'll enjoy this timely and practical series!

Dr. Kevin Leman

Author, *Sheet Music: Uncovering the Secrets of
Sexual Intimacy in Marriage*

The *Focus on the Family Marriage Series* is successful because it shifts
the focus from how to fix or strengthen a marriage to *who* can do it.
Through this study you will learn that a blessed marriage will be the
happy by-product of a closer relationship with the *creator* of marriage.

Lisa Whelchel

Author, *Creative Correction* and
The Facts of Life and Other Lessons My Father Taught Me

In a day and age where the covenant of marriage is so quickly tossed
aside in the name of incompatibility and irreconcilable differences, a
marriage Bible study that is both inspirational and practical is desperately
needed. The *Focus on the Family Marriage Series* is what couples are seeking.
I give my highest recommendation to this Bible study series that has the
potential to dramatically impact and improve marriages today. Marriage
is not so much about finding the right partner as it is about being the
right partner. These studies give wonderful biblical teachings for
helping those who want to learn the beautiful art of being and
becoming all that God intends in their marriage.

Lysa TerKeurst

President, Proverbs 31 Ministries
Author, *Capture His Heart* and *Capture Her Heart*

focus on the family® marriage series

the
covenant
marriage

Gospel Light

Gospel Light is an evangelical Christian publisher dedicated to serving the local church. We believe God's vision for Gospel Light is to provide church leaders with biblical, user-friendly materials that will help them evangelize, disciple and minister to children, youth and families.

It is our prayer that this Gospel Light resource will help you discover biblical truth for your own life and help you minister to others. May God richly bless you.

For a free catalog of resources from Gospel Light, please call your Christian supplier or contact us at 1-800-4-GOSPEL *or* www.gospellight.com

PUBLISHING STAFF
William T. Greig, Chairman
Kyle Duncan, Publisher
Dr. Elmer L. Towns, Senior Consulting Publisher
Pam Weston, Senior Editor
Patti Pennington Virtue, Associate Editor
Hilary Young, Editorial Assistant
Bayard Taylor, M.Div., Senior Editor, Biblical and Theological Issues
Samantha A. Hsu, Cover and Internal Designer
Christi Goeser, Contributing Writer

ISBN 0-8307-3119-9
© 2003 Focus on the Family
All rights reserved.
Printed in the U.S.A.

table of contents

foreword

The most urgent mission field on Earth is not across the sea or even across the street—it's right where you live: in your home and family. Jesus' last instruction was to "make disciples of all nations" (Matthew 28:19). At the thought of this command, our eyes look across the world for our work field. That's not bad; it's just not *all*. God intended the home to be the first place of Christian discipleship and growth (see Deuteronomy 6:4-8). Our family members must be the *first* ones we reach out to in word and example with the gospel of the Lord Jesus Christ, and the fundamental way in which this occurs is through the marriage relationship.

Divorce, blended families, the breakdown of communication and the complexities of daily life are taking a devastating toll on the God-ordained institutions of marriage and family. We do not need to look hard or search far for evidence that even Christian marriages and families are also in a desperate state. In response to the need to build strong Christ-centered marriages and families, this series was developed.

Focus on the Family is well known and respected worldwide for its steadfast dedication to preserving the sanctity of marriage and family life. I can think of no better partnership than the one formed by Focus on the Family and Gospel Light to produce the *Focus on the Family Marriage Series*. This series is well-written, biblically sound and right on target for guiding couples to explore the foundation God has laid for marriage and to see Him as the role model for the perfect spouse. Through these studies, seeds will be planted that will germinate in your heart and mind for many years to come.

In our practical, bottom-line culture, we often want to jump over the *why* and get straight to the *what*. We think that by *doing* the six steps or *learning* the five ways, we will reach the goal. But deep-rooted growth is slower and more purposeful and begins with a well-grounded understanding of God's divine design. Knowing why marriage exists is crucial to making the how-tos more effective. Marriage is a gift from God, a unique and distinct covenant relationship through which His glory and goodness can resonate, and it is only through knowing the architect and His plan that we will build our marriage on the surest foundation.

God created marriage; He has a specific purpose for it, and He is committed to filling with fresh life and renewed strength each union yielded to Him. God wants to gather the hearts of every couple together, unite them in love and walk them to the finish line—all in His great grace and goodness.

May God, in His grace, lead you into His truth, strengthening your lives and your marriage.

Gary T. Smalley
Founder and Chairman of the Board
Smalley Relationship Center

introduction

*At the beginning of creation God "made them male and female." "For this
reason a man will leave his father and mother and be united to his wife,
and the two will become one flesh." So they are no longer two, but one.*
Mark 10:6-8

The Covenant Marriage can be used in a variety of situations, including small-
group Bible studies, Sunday School classes or counseling or mentoring
situations. An individual couple can also use this book as an at-home
marriage-building study.

Each of the four sessions contains four main components.

Session Overview

Tilling the Ground
This is an introduction to the topic being discussed—commentary and questions to direct your thoughts toward the main idea of the session.

Planting the Seed
This is the Bible study portion in which you will read Scripture and answer
questions to help discover lasting truths from God's Word.

Watering the Hope
This is a time for discussion and prayer. Whether you are using the study at
home as a couple, in a small group or in a classroom setting, talking about
the lesson with your spouse is a great way to solidify the truth and plant it
deeply into your hearts.

Harvesting the Fruit
As a point of action, this portion of the session offers suggestions on putting
the truth of the Word into action in your marriage relationship.

Suggestions for Individual Couple Study

There are at least three options for using this study as a couple.

- It may be used as a devotional study that each spouse would study individually through the week; then on a specified day, come together and discuss what you have learned and how to apply it to your marriage.
- You might choose to study one session together in an evening and then work on the application activities during the rest of the week.
- Because of the short length of this study, it is a great resource for a weekend retreat. Take a trip away for the weekend, and study each session together, interspersed with your favorite leisure activities.

Suggestions for Group Study

There are many ways that this study can be used in a group situation. The most common way is in a small-group Bible study format. However, it can also be used in adult Sunday School class. However you choose to use it, there are some general guidelines to follow for group study.

- Keep the group small—five to six couples is probably the maximum.
- Ask couples to commit to regular attendance for the four weeks of the study. Regular attendance is a key to building relationships and trust in a group.
- Encourage participants *not* to share anything of a personal or potentially embarrassing nature without first asking the spouse's permission.
- Whatever is discussed in the group meetings is to be held in strictest confidence among group members only.

There are additional leader helps in the back of this book and in *The Focus on the Family Marriage Ministry Guide.*

Suggestions for Mentoring or Counseling Relationships

This study also lends itself for use in relationships where one couple mentors or counsels another couple.

- A mentoring relationship, where a couple that has been married for several years is assigned to meet on a regular basis with a younger couple, could be arranged through a system set up by a church or ministry.
- A less formal way to start a mentoring relationship is for a younger couple to take the initiative and approach a couple that exemplify a mature, godly marriage and ask them to meet with them on a regular basis. Or the reverse might be a mature couple that approaches a younger couple to begin a mentoring relationship.
- When asked to mentor, some might shy away and think that they could never do that, knowing that their own marriage is less than perfect. But just as we are to disciple new believers, we must learn to disciple married couples to strengthen marriages in this difficult world. The Lord has promised to be "with you always" (Matthew 28:20).
- Before you begin to mentor a couple, first complete the study yourselves. This will serve to strengthen your own marriage and prepare you for leading another couple.
- Be prepared to learn as much or more than the couple(s) you will mentor.

There are additional helps for mentoring relationships in the *The Focus on the Family Marriage Ministry Guide.*

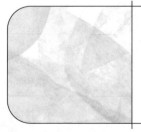

The Focus on the Family Marriage Series *is based on Al Janssen's* The Marriage Masterpiece *(Wheaton, IL: Tyndale House Publishers, 2001), an insightful look at what marriage can—and should—be. In this study, we are pleased to lead you through the wonderful journey of discovering the joy in your marriage that God wants you to experience!*

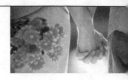

the role model

I gave you my solemn oath and entered into covenant with you,
declares the Sovereign LORD, and you became mine.
Ezekiel 16:8

As the first couple, Adam and Eve offer us a glimpse of how God designed marriage to be. When we look at how this first couple was made and what they were commissioned to do, we gain an understanding of what God has created and suited us for as well.

Adam and Eve had it good—to put it mildly. The Garden of Eden was a beautiful place. There, in the wonder of the amazing world around them, they enjoyed not only the company of each other but also fellowship with God, their Father and guide. But instead of enjoying this paradise and fulfilling their commission, they sinned (see Genesis 3). We can see how their sin dropped as a veil over God's purpose for their lives to the point where we now see His intention "through a glass, darkly" (1 Corinthians 13:12, *KJV*). However, our great and merciful God did not leave mankind to flounder in this state of darkened brokenness. Instead, He provided an example of what a marital relationship can be. How? By giving us the ultimate role model—Himself!

The positive and negative examples of marriage that were set before us as children helped shape our understanding of what this powerful, God-ordained relationship should be. We were influenced not only by our own families but also by the families of our friends and even media-portrayed marriages.

1. What kinds of role models for marriage did you have while growing up?

2. In whom did you find your most influential role model for marriage while you were growing up?

3. What positive qualities were demonstrated in this marriage relationship?

4. What negative qualities were demonstrated?

5. How did this example of a marriage relationship shape your ideas about what a marriage can be?

6. At this point in your marriage, who are your strongest role models for marriage? Why?

In this fallen world of imperfection, we still have a perfect role model. God shines the truest love and reveals the perfect intention for what marriage can be. You have only to gaze at God's marriage to His people to discover His heart for His beloved. Allow His truth to carefully remove the years of residue accumulated by poor instruction or ignorance, and reclaim what is yours by His gracious gift—a marriage relationship that echoes His own, revealing His glory and goodness.

planting the seed

It may be odd to think of God as married, but the Bible makes it clear that He is. As you study the following passages, think about this: Marriage is meant to be a human relationship that reflects God's commitment to us. Marriage between a man and a woman is the echo of the love God has voiced to His people.

Our Marriage Model

7. By what names or titles is God referred to in Isaiah 54:5?

8. What character qualities do these names or titles connote?

9. How do these character qualities reflect God's commitment to His people as a husband?

God desired an intimate relationship with His people, so He took a proactive stand; He initiated the relationship and pledged Himself as a faithful and committed husband.

Ezekiel 16:8-14 is an allegory of God's relationship with His chosen people.

10. List what God did for His people according to Ezekiel 16:8-14.

11. Compare this passage with the mandate given to husbands in Ephesians 5:25-27.

A husband takes the initiative to protect and adorn his wife. God was proactive when it came to His treatment of His Bride. As creator, God made His people; as husband, He blessed and adorned them by pouring upon them His protection and guidance.

12. Compare Ruth 3:9 to Ezekiel 16:8. Both verses talk about spreading the corner of a garment over someone. What do you think was the significance of this act?

The spreading of a corner of a man's garment over a woman was symbolic of entering into a marriage covenant. It expressed both protection and intimacy, just as God initiated a relationship with His people and drew them into His divine protection. Consider the words that God spoke to His people, "I gave you my solemn oath and entered into covenant with you . . . and you became mine" (Ezekiel 16:8). God was not merely creating people and leaving them to fend for themselves. This was not a casual or distant relationship. He desired fellowship and communion with them that only they—beings created in His image (see Genesis 1:26-27)—could experience. The words "entered into a covenant" indicate an unbreakable bond—something that, once enacted, could not be dissolved except at penalty of death. God had forever linked Himself to His Bride!

13. Read Malachi 2:16. Why do you think God hates divorce?

14. How does the idea of divorce stand in direct contrast to God's foundational design for marriage?

The idea of God as husband in the Old Testament provides a basis for the New Testament teaching that Christ is the Bridegroom and the Church is His Bride. Second Corinthians 11:2; Ephesians 5:31-33 and Revelation 19:7-9 give more details of this relationship between the Bridegroom and His Bride and how it relates to marriage.

15. What is characteristic of the Bride in each of these passages?

16. What does God expect of His Bride?

17. What kind of husband is God?

Foundational Characteristics of Marriage

We can identify at least three traits of God as a spouse to His people. These foundational characteristics give us a solid role model for responding in our own marriage relationships.

Be Proactive

God took the initiative to bring our relationship with Him into being, not only as our creator, but as the One who cleansed and adorned His people.

18. In what ways are you proactive, rather than passive, in your own marriage relationship?

19. In which areas could you be more proactive?

Love Unconditionally

God's response of love was not based upon the actions of His people, but upon His nature as One who gives Himself to His Bride with no strings attached.

20. What does it mean to show unconditional love?

21. Describe a time when your spouse demonstrated unconditional love toward you.

Be Faithful

God was true to His word and kept reaching out to His people, even when they turned their backs on Him.

22. How can you better cultivate the character trait of faithfulness in your marriage?

23. Break the word "faithful" into its parts, and you'll end up with "faith" and "full." How does being full of faith promote a lasting marriage?

Think about the statement, "Your Maker is your husband" (Isaiah 54:5). Does it draw your thoughts back to that lush and pristine Garden of Eden— to the time and place where God's presence permeated creation and united Adam and Eve as one?

Marriage is the metaphor—the example—through which we are instructed about an even deeper relationship: the marriage of God to His people. Too often we look at marriage as the reality that can teach us about God, rather than seeing that God is the reality who teaches us about Himself through our human experience of marriage.

24. Why did God "marry" His people, and what do you think He desires from this relationship?

25. How does God's example of proactive faithfulness give us the definitive role model for our marriage?

26. The Church is called the Bride of Christ. What does this truth mean to you personally?

27. What does the picture of Christ and His Bride, the Church, say to you about how God might view your marriage?

harvesting the fruit

28. Discuss with your spouse the attributes of God that make Him a good model for marriage. Make a list of your observations from the Scriptures and what you've learned in this session.

Now choose the three most important attributes in your list and state how you will apply them to your life.

This week make it a daily point of prayer, both individually and as a couple, to ask for God's help in seeing these qualities develop more fully in each of you and in your marriage.

Make a dinner date for the end of the week! During the dinner, use specific events from the week to share how you saw God answer your prayers. Although our growth into spiritually mature Christians is an ongoing journey, it is important to take time to encourage and affirm the positive steps you are taking along the way. Share with your spouse what you admire most in him or her, and commit again as a couple to becoming all that God wants you to be.

the betrothal

I will betroth you to me forever; I will betroth you
in righteousness and justice, in love and compassion.
I will betroth you in faithfulness, and you will acknowledge the Lord.
Hosea 2:19-20

When *did* God get betrothed? Seems an odd question, doesn't it? After all, there is no chapter and verse to point to and say, "Aha! *This* is when He popped the question."

Many people aren't comfortable with the whole idea of God being married and consider this to be a literary term—not meant to be taken literally. But although He isn't married in the same sense that you and your spouse are, neither is the imagery of God's marriage to His people just distant allegory. It is a true and poignant portrait of our maker-redeemer as a faithful and compassionate husband whose love for His Bride models what true love can be.

God knows how this all works because He not only created the marriage relationship, but He also gave us an example of it in His own marriage to His people. It is in this way that we can come to understand how marriage is meant to work: God Himself has painted the picture for us.

Marriage proposals come in all shapes and sizes; some are richly adorned events; others are simple and straightforward. Some are lengthy and passionate; others are off-the-cuff and impetuous. Think back to your marriage proposal.

1. How and when did you and your spouse get engaged?

2. Describe the actual marriage proposal.

3. What promises did you make to each other when the proposal occurred?

4. What does it mean to be engaged to someone?

5. In your opinion, how binding is an engagement?

Becoming engaged is a pivotal point in the relationship between a man and a woman, but the biblical concept of betrothal was even more binding.

planting the seed

We must first define what betrothal really is and how it is different from the present practice of engagement. A modern-day engagement is more like a testing period to see if the man and woman really want to go through with a marriage. It is a proving time, when final decisions regarding the future are made, but it is not a binding agreement.

This isn't all bad. Certainly an engagement is a period for solidifying future plans and further defining where our commitments are taking us. But in biblical times, a betrothal was much more formal and legally binding. It was a ceremony that, like marriage, could not be dissolved except by divorce or death. A betrothal was a *covenant*. It wasn't just saying "I'll try," but rather "I *do*."

6. An example of the seriousness of the betrothal covenant in biblical times is found in Matthew 1:18-19. What was Joseph going to do and why?

Joseph could, by law, have had Mary judged publicly as an adulteress and stoned, even though they were not yet married. That is how serious the betrothal was taken in biblical days. We can look back to specific times when God initiated a covenant—a betrothal—with His people.

7. In Genesis 12:1-3 what did God instruct Abram to do?

8. What did God promise to do for Abram?

This first encounter between God and Abram marked a new beginning for human history. Once again, the God of the universe was revealing Himself and His plan for making a people for Himself. Although the covenant was specifically made between God and Abram, the New Testament makes it clear that we become partakers of that covenant through faith in Christ (see Galatians 3:6-9).

God spoke to Abram, a man of no renown who lived in an idolatrous and pagan culture, telling him to leave his city and begin a journey. There was no firm destination, no clear point of arrival; only a promise of rich and abundant blessing.

9. In what ways is a betrothal similar to Abram's experience of journeying to a new land?

10. How does Genesis 12:1 compare with the instructions given to Adam and Eve in Genesis 2:24?

11. Why is leaving and cleaving important?

Abram made the journey God requested, and along the way God continued to affirm His promises.

12. What did God affirm to Abram in Genesis 12:6-7 and 13:14-18?

13. What was Abram's response?

14. In what way did you reaffirm your commitment to your future spouse during your engagement?

15. How was your relationship strengthened during your engagement?

Settled and prosperous, Abram again met with divine revelation when God appeared, confirming His covenant promise with Abram and his descendants. This time, however, Abram inquired of the Lord as to how He was planning to make him a great nation (see Genesis 15:2-3). God answered. Abram believed. A ceremony sealed the agreement. Read about the ceremony in Genesis 15:1-21.

16. Describe the covenant ceremony that occurred between God and Abram (vv. 9-12,17-18).

17. What was agreed upon in this covenant?

It is necessary to have further explanation to understand what was meant by this ceremony. In ancient times, when two tribes made a treaty or when a boy and girl were betrothed in marriage, a legally binding ceremony was performed to emphasize the seriousness of the covenant that was being entered into. The two parties to the agreement would each sacrifice an animal, spilling its blood on the ground. They would then walk barefoot through the blood as a living illustration of what would happen to either of them should they fail to keep their part of the agreement. In other words, if one of the parties broke the promise, or covenant, he would forfeit his life.[1]

What is unusual about the covenant ceremony between God and Abram described in Genesis 15 is that only the Lord—in the form of the firepot with the torch—passed through the blood while Abram had fallen into a deep slumber. Although it may seem an insignificant detail at first, it is really a huge statement about God's commitment to the covenant. By walking alone, God was declaring Himself responsible if *either* party of the agreement broke the covenant. Though they were both bound by the agreement, God assumed liability for either party violating the promise.

What a picture of the grace of God that not only did He initiate the covenant, but He also promised to uphold both ends of it—even if it meant sacrificing His life. As New Testament believers, we can see how Jesus' death upon the cross was rightfully our punishment for breaking the covenant.

How does this relate to marriage? It provides us with the perfect picture of both the solemnity and depth of a betrothal commitment. God called Abram and made a covenant with him that was binding, and He was willing to put His life on the line to see it fulfilled. In our marriage, we must make a commitment for which we are willing to lay down our lives.

Throughout Scripture God's desire for His chosen people is that they be completely His—belonging to no one else, exclusively and eternally bound to Him through the power of His Spirit and Word. The picture of God as husband and believers as His Bride, and the eventual wedding supper of the Lamb, is not heretical or even mildly divergent. It is truth—a reality that we can enjoy now and forever.

18. Read Hosea 2:19-20. List the ways in which God was committing Himself to His Bride.

19. How has your spouse demonstrated any of these traits in his or her commitment to you?

Hosea 2:19-20 shows us that betrothal is followed by acknowledging the Lord. A betrothal is a full and complete commitment to someone and is intended to lead us to a place of deeper intimacy. When we think of marriage in this light and consider how God betrothed Himself to His chosen people, we can see that our covenant with our intended spouse is not a testing period; it is the specific beginning of a committed relationship that will result in a shared and fruitful life.

watering the hope

Love can be offered, but it can't be demanded. Even after Abram responded to God's call and set out for a new land, there were times when uncertainty and doubt crowded his vision. But through it all, Abram was commended by God for his faith (see Genesis 15:6; Romans 4:3; Galatians 3:6; James 2:23). He believed God, and his faith carried him through.

Like Abram, our choice to love must at some point be upheld by faith. When we commit our lives to another, we are taking a chance—but we are *not* doomed to failure. Marriage can last a lifetime; it can work and blossom into a rich and rewarding relationship of deep intimacy and blessing.

20. When you got engaged, did you consider it to be as binding as a wedding ceremony? Why or why not?

21. How long should an engagement last?

22. What is the purpose of an engagement?

23. What should be the goal of a man and a woman who become engaged?

24. Today many people make prenuptial agreements before they are married. How is this similar to the biblical idea of covenant?

How is it different?

25. In light of what you've learned, has your perception of the meaning of "covenant" changed? If so, how?

26. How is becoming engaged an act of faith?

harvesting the fruit

Understanding how committed God is to you personally is necessary for you to express that same commitment to your spouse.

27. How does the example of God's covenant with Abram demonstrate His love and commitment to His chosen people?

What does this say to you about God's love and commitment to you today?

28. How can you demonstrate a similar commitment to your spouse?

Spend a few moments in prayer, asking God to reveal afresh His commitment to you and also to help you express that same commitment to your spouse.

Plan to reenact your marriage proposal this week, as much as possible. If you cannot exactly reenact it, at least plan a romantic dinner out or a quiet evening at home—alone. The important idea is that you think through what you want to say and how you want to say it beforehand by considering the following:

- *What are the necessary components of a covenant?*
- *How will I demonstrate the commitment I am making?*
- *How binding is my commitment?*

After your date, seal your proposal with prayer for God's refreshing and blessing over your marriage and for the grace to keep your promises to each other.

Note

1. Ray Vander Laan and Judith E. Markham, *Echoes of His Presence* (Colorado Springs, CO: Focus on the Family, 1996), pp. 6-7.

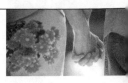

the
ceremony

Let us rejoice and be glad and give him glory!
For the wedding of the Lamb has come,
and his bride has made herself ready.
Revelation 19:7

The business of putting together weddings is a huge and profitable industry. Magazines, TV programs, bridal fairs, books and websites by the hundreds have surfaced to ensure that all the details of a couple's special day are done right and done well. From the right color of ribbon for the reception place cards to the types of flowers in the bride's bouquet to the best kind of filling in the wedding cake, couples have a plethora of voices offering opinions, advice and options—and each couple will spend an average of over $20,000 to see that all the loose ends are tied up neatly and everything comes out picture-perfect.

When did getting married get so complicated? Have we lost something in the process of trying to create the picture-perfect day? Weddings are, without a doubt, one of the most significant and life-changing events a man and woman will ever experience—but have we focused on the trees so intently that we can no longer see the forest? When everything is said and done, what's a wedding really all about?

tilling the ground

Whether you've been married for decades or for less than a year, your wedding day is likely to be etched into your memory with a distinction and clarity rarely given to other past events.

1. How long did you take to plan your wedding?

2. Who did most of the planning?

3. How did you decide what elements to include in your ceremony?

4. What was the single most important element of your wedding ceremony?

5. What unexpected or funny thing happened?

6. In what ways did your ceremony mirror your understanding of marriage?

So much goes in to a wedding ceremony: time, money, energy, expectations, emotions, etc. In this session we will discover how the foundation for marriage—its very purpose—is revealed through the ceremony itself.

planting the seed

Most wedding ceremonies are built around traditions. Is there a biblical basis for these time-honored rituals? If so, what do these traditions say about the intention for marriage? Most important, can we find where God is a role model for the ceremony too?

There are several key points found in the covenant between Abram and God that shed light on some of our own wedding traditions and help us to see their importance as symbols of the true purpose for marriage.

An Act of Faith

Entering into a marriage relationship requires an act of faith. We begin marriage without knowing or understanding how everything will work out; but we have heartfelt confidence and commitment to our spouse that speaks deep inside, quietly anchoring our soul to our marriage partner in patient faith.

This faith is modeled in the initial covenant made between God and Abram as seen in Genesis 12:1-5 and can be a starting point for us today.

7. What were God's instructions to Abram in Genesis 12:1-5?

What were the blessings He promised to Abram?

Abram acknowledged the Lord as the true and living God, and in obedience to God's call, Abram left his home to journey to a new land. Unlike his culture's prevailing belief in polytheism—worship of many gods—Abram rejected the idols being venerated as gods and only worshiped the one true God.

8. What statement is made in relation to marriage in Genesis 2:24?

9. In what ways are Genesis 12:1 and 2:24 similar?

It must have taken a great deal of faith for Abram to set out toward an unknown destination across the desert on the basis of the promises of a relatively unknown God. Not only did he follow God's instructions to him, but he also convinced his wife, his nephew and their servants to go along!

10. How much of a role does faith play in an engagement and a marriage commitment?

11. In what ways does faith stabilize your relationship now?

A New Name

One of the open demonstrations of the seriousness of a faith commitment to each other is seen when God gives Abram a new name in Genesis 17:5.

12. In what context is Abram given this new name (Genesis 17:1-9)?

13. Why is this significant?

   Abram received a new name from God, signifying the great purpose to which God had called him. By accepting his new name, Abram was showing his faith in God and his submission to Him.

   After a marriage in our culture, a woman traditionally takes her husband's surname to signify oneness. It is a symbolic gesture showing that the woman is submitting herself to her husband, allowing her life to be identified with his.

14. How important is it that a woman take her husband's surname?

In what circumstances might a woman wish to retain her maiden name?

15. If a woman chooses to retain her maiden name, is she sending a message that she is not fully committed to her husband or that she is not willing to identify her life with her husband's life? Explain your answer.

Whether or not a woman takes her husband's last name is a very personal choice that must be made by each couple.

A Symbol

As a symbol of the covenant made between Abraham and God, Abraham and all the men in his household were circumcised. In this way, they would be reminded daily of the promises that had been made in their covenant with God.

16. What was the purpose of circumcision according to Genesis 17:10–14?

Just as Abraham and his household received a physical reminder of the covenant made with God, a wedding ring is much more significant than just a symbol to show outsiders that you and your spouse are taken. A wedding ring is a tangible, daily reminder of the binding covenant you share with your spouse.

17. In what way might your wedding ring be a reminder of the covenant you made with your spouse?

The Fruit

New life flows from an intimate relationship. "What about those couples who choose not to have children or those who cannot have children?" you may ask. The answer is that new life can flow not only from having children and bringing them up to be men and women of God, but also from bringing others into God's family and nurturing them in the faith. When you have children, you bring new life into your family; when you witness to others, you bring new life into the family of God.

18. What was the promised blessing of Genesis 12:2-3 (repeated in 13:16; 15:5-6; 17:2,6-7; 22:17)?

How does this blessing relate to spiritual fruitfulness?

19. Why is nurturing new life an important part of a marriage relationship?

Though God's dealings with Abraham were not an official wedding ceremony, we can see through the similarities outlined in this session that they hold great meaning and purpose for us today. The elements we consider most vital to a wedding ceremony are, in fact, elements that flow from the true intention of marriage. God provided a model for us so that we could understand what weddings are meant to be. A wedding is much more than a party; it is an act of faith that unites two into one.

The Ceremony

Let's look more closely at some of the elements of a traditional wedding ceremony and compare them with the biblical concept of covenant to see how those elements draw us to a deeper understanding of marriage.

We Gather in the Sight of God

"Dearly beloved, we are gathered here in the sight of God . . ." Most of us have heard these words or something similar at a wedding. It is an absolutely true statement; a wedding ceremony *is* conducted before God. OK, OK, so everything we do is in the sight of God; He is omnipresent. But what is the significance of making a marriage covenant before God?

When a man and a woman present themselves before God in their wedding ceremony, they are declaring that their relationship is submitted and accountable to Him.

20. Did you consciously invite God's presence into your wedding ceremony, submitting your union to Him? Why or why not?

21. How have you continued to invite God's presence into your marriage?

We Invite Witnesses to the Ceremony

Another element present in both weddings and in covenants is that there are witnesses to the exchange. Why is this important? Because it compels those making the commitments accountable to follow through with the promises they made.

Ideally, those who witness a wedding are there to support the couple not only as they embark on their journey but also as the years progress. These witnesses are to come alongside and challenge the couple to remain true to their vows during times of struggle and hardship. These friends and family members pick up the slack when a couple needs extra help and rejoice as that couple grows stronger and more mature.

22. Who were the witnesses to your marriage ceremony?

23. How have these people kept you accountable to your vows?

We Declare Our Commitment

The centerpiece of a wedding ceremony or a covenant is the exchanging of vows. These vows are not just words to be recited, but they are the unconditional declaration of the commitment being made. Just as God declared His intent and His commitment to Abram, and Abram reciprocated by declaring his faith and following through in obedience, so it is with wedding vows. The man first states his intention to love and support his bride through thick and thin. The woman reciprocates by making the same or similar commitment to her groom. There are no qualifiers or disclaimers; each party makes an irrevocable vow and assumes full responsibility for the marriage.

24. What specific vows did you make to your spouse?

25. How did your vows compare to the instructions given to husbands and wives in Ephesians 5:22-29?

We Exchange Something of Value

Typically after vows are made, a gift is given to prove the sincerity and to be a physical reminder of the promises that have been made. God gave Abraham land—a place that would become an inheritance for his descendants. This land was much more than just the soil and vegetation: It meant permanence and security for Abraham.

Wedding rings are similar in that they are a constant and costly reminder of the seriousness and dedication that a man and woman are bringing into their marriage. The act of giving is an open display of what has happened inside their hearts. They are committing themselves to give all of themselves to each other.

26. How does exchanging gifts—whether wedding rings or something else—demonstrate your commitment to your spouse?

27. What would you like your spouse to think of when he or she sees the ring (or other gift) you gave to him or her?

28. What does a marriage ceremony tell us about the commitment being made?

29. What do you think most people understand to be the purpose of a wedding ceremony?

30. Does understanding the seriousness of a covenant change the way you view a marriage ceremony? How?

harvesting the fruit

Share your answers to questions 20 through 27 with your spouse and then discuss the following questions together:

31. What elements of your ceremony really underscored your intention for marriage?

32. If you were planning your wedding again, what would you do differently?

During this week, think about how the exchange of rings at your wedding represented the giving of your life to your spouse and vice versa. Pray about what you could give to your spouse at this point in your marriage to express your continued commitment. This doesn't have to be something that costs a lot of money—just something that would be a meaningful and deliberate way to once again say that you are giving your life in covenant to your spouse. Plan a specific time right now when you will exchange these symbols of renewed commitment.

Close in prayer, thanking God for bringing you and your spouse together and inviting Him to be the center of your covenant. Ask for His inspiration in coming up with a symbolic gift to renew your covenant marriage.

the commitment

They are no longer two, but one.
Therefore what God has joined together, let man not separate.
Matthew 19:6

In 1997, the state of Louisiana made a bold step toward helping couples consider the seriousness of a marriage commitment. The state gave couples two options when it came to getting married: (1) apply for a standard contract marriage under no-fault divorce laws or (2) apply for a covenant marriage that allows for divorce only on limited grounds and only after waiting a period of one year. Most couples chose the standard contract, but an increasingly growing number of couples have gravitated toward the covenant.[1] The outcome? Covenant marriages significantly outlast contract marriages.[2]

A marriage commitment in its truest form is a covenant—a serious agreement for which there is no escape mechanism or back door for a quick exit. Until we think of marriage in this light, we will be tempted to consider leaving when things get tough (and no matter how great the marriage, things *will* get tough sometimes!). God's covenant with Abram is our model for marriage, and through this example, we can learn how committed a marriage partnership should be. The words "for better, for worse . . . until death do us part" in your wedding vows leave no room for divorce. Your marriage may seem one-sided at times; it may feel unbearably difficult at others; it will mean a lot of sacrifice, but your lifelong commitment to the marriage God ordained is no more than God Himself has promised to you.

tilling the ground

It's not news to any of us: Divorce rates have risen sharply over the past few decades. No-fault divorce laws, increasing financial equality for women and the pervasive value of personal fulfillment at all costs have paved the way for easier and less cumbersome breakups. In today's culture, it seems as if marriage is meant to last only as long as the husband and wife feel like it. Then, as if trading in an old car, married couples feel the desire to make a change and find something—or someone—new.

1. While growing up, did you expect the marriages around you (your parents, your grandparents, your aunts and uncles, the parents of friends, etc.) to last a lifetime? Which did last a lifetime? How many did not?

2. How has divorce affected your own life?

3. Why is it hard for couples to stay in their marriages?

As we consider the commitment of marriage, we must keep in mind the truths we have already studied because these truths are the reasons we hold fast to our promises.

Truth One

Marriage is a gift from God, designed to reflect His image to the world.

Truth Two

Marriage is not merely about finding personal happiness and fulfillment; it is also a place of selfless love that seeks to emulate God's own selfless love for us.

Truth Three

Marriage is the human relationship that demonstrates God's own commitment to us.

Divorce is not God's plan for any marriage because it severs a bond that He intends to use as a point of grace and a reflection of glory that represents a part of Himself to the world.

planting the seed

What is the real cost of a wedding? Much more than money, it is a covenant that binds two lives together as one—an act of divine unity that is meant to last a lifetime. Many wonder if it can be done. Can a marriage last a lifetime? Scripture cries out a resounding YES! Though it is not always easy or comfortable, God has both instructed and modeled how marriage can last forever.

Uprooting Wrong Ideas

Before you can plant a garden, you must prepare the soil by uprooting anything that may potentially become destructive to what you are planting. Getting the weeds out—roots and all—is vital to a fruitful harvest. Likewise, before you can focus on strengthening your commitment to your spouse, there are attitudes that may need to be uprooted from your thinking in order to give your marriage commitment a chance to really thrive. Some of these ideas are a review of what was studied in the first study of this series,

The Masterpiece Marriage. If you have not completed that study, you may find it beneficial to do so.

Unrealistic Expectations

One of the causes of trouble in marriage is the unrealistic expectations for what married life should be like that each spouse brings into the relationship.

4. As you were growing up, what was your expectation for how your married life would be?

5. How has our culture influenced our expectations of marriage?

Unclear Purposes

When spouses have opposing goals for their marriage, there will be additional friction.

6. What does our culture seem to understand as the primary purpose for marriage?

7. What do you believe is God's purpose for marriage?

8. Why did you get married?

Uncertain Commitment

Because some couples have unrealistic expectations and an unclear understanding of God's purpose for marriage, they also believe that their commitment is conditional.

9. How does society contribute to the idea that a marriage commitment is not permanently binding?

If our primary expectation in marriage is for personal happiness, then our relationship is based upon our feelings—which can change—and not on a binding commitment—a covenant—with our spouse. When conflict arises or the feelings change, we might feel justified to end the relationship. But God has a better plan.

Planting Right Ideas

How can we have realistic, purposeful and committed marriages? Let's consider what God's Word has to say about the marriage commitment.

10. What do the following Scripture passages say about the God-ordained union between a man and a woman?

Genesis 1:27

Genesis 2:24

11. What did Jesus say about the importance of marriage according to Matthew 19:3-6 (also according to Mark 10:6-9)?

"But what if I married the wrong person?" someone might ask. If anyone had the right to walk away from a covenant, it was God. Consider the numerous and continuous ways in which His chosen people, whom He loved and favored, rejected His ways and blatantly disobeyed His Word; yet He continued to keep His commitment.

12. What do the following passages say about God's commitment to His Bride—His people?

    Isaiah 54:5-8

    Ezekiel 16:59-60,62-63

    Hosea 14:1-2,4

13. How would you relate God's example of a fully committed spouse to dealing with a troubled earthly marriage?

Many couples fail to realize that marriage is a covenant, one that stands unwavering even when feelings change or circumstances become difficult. The covenant ensures ongoing, growing relationship, rather than bondage. It is meant to be a blessing and a point of security. When couples eliminate the option of divorce from their minds and accept that their covenant is not dissolvable except through death, then they will be able to navigate the hard times without jumping ship.

God's grace is sufficient to redeem our bad decisions and to make something beautiful out of our lives—this includes what may seem like a wrong marriage.

Is Divorce Ever Permissible?

Divorce was never a part of God's plan for marriage; however, God allowed divorce under certain conditions.

14. In Matthew 19:3, when the Pharisees asked Jesus "Is it lawful for a man to divorce his wife *for any and every reason?*"(emphasis added), what was His answer (vv. 4-6)?

15. As you continue to read of Jesus' conversation with the Pharisees, notice the subtle change of words as you fill in the following blanks:

    " 'Why then,' [the Pharisees] asked, 'did Moses _____ that a man give his wife a certificate of divorce and send her away?' " (v. 7).

    "Jesus replied, 'Moses _____ you to divorce your wives because your hearts were hard. But it was not this way from the beginning. I tell you that any one who divorces his wife, except for marital unfaithfulness, and marries another woman commits adultery.' "(vv. 8-9).

    What does the subtle change in words and Jesus' reply tell you about the Pharisees' intent? Was permissible divorce the issue, or was there perhaps another purpose for their query?

    Marriage is intended to be a covenant relationship in which we extend ourselves beyond our personal rights and seek to allow God's grace to mold and shape us into His divine image. What about marriages in which violence (or the threat of violence), degradation or humiliation exists? Does the Bible require that the abused partner stick with the marriage because the marriage covenant is unconditional?

16. In your opinion, how might physical or emotional abuse, neglect or abandonment be considered lack of faithfulness to one's spouse?

When it is all said and done, a marriage commitment must be viewed as unconditional—unconditional surrender and faithfulness to another person. It is a relationship where we extend ourselves beyond our rights and seek to allow God's grace to mold and shape us into His divine image. When abuse in any form undermines this unconditional surrender, the abuser is effectively denying the image of God in his or her spouse.

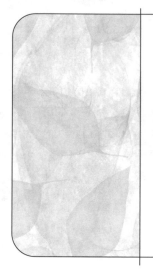

*A **note to those who've been through divorce:** There are many reasons why some marriages fail. Perhaps there is no specific problem at which you can point your finger and say, "This is the reason my marriage didn't work out." Perhaps you were previously in a marriage where God's presence wasn't invited into the relationship, and without that solid foundation, the marriage simply fell apart. For whatever reasons your previous marriage failed, you can have the marriage God intended this time around. Accept God's forgiveness for past failures and make a covenant commitment to your spouse today. You'll be on your way to enjoying marriage as God intended—a relationship with Him as the foundation.*

Consider the following story:

> After 12 years of what seemed to be a happy marriage and shortly after the birth of their third child, Sarah discovered that her husband, Jason, had been having an affair with a coworker for at least a year. When she confronted him with the evidence, he at first denied it but then confessed when he saw her evidence: a year's worth of credit-card receipts for places Sarah had never been and gifts she had never received. Jason begged for forgiveness and promised to go to counseling sessions with their pastor to save the marriage. After two months, however, Sarah realized that he was continuing to see the other woman. Jason made repeated, tearful vows to stop seeing his coworker, but then he began blaming Sarah for his need to seek love elsewhere. Finally, Sarah asked him to move out of the house, and she began to consider her options. Her pastor advised her that divorce was not part of God's plan; her parents told her to dump Jason, think of the children and get on with her life; her friends seemed to avoid her. The irony of it all was that she still loved her husband—wondering what she had done to drive him away—and she missed him terribly![3]

17. If Sarah and Jason were your friends, what could you do to help them?

How could this marriage be saved?

18. In the case of infidelity the Bible says divorce is allowable, but is divorce the only option? Explain.

In what other situations might divorce be justified?

How can God redeem troubled marriages and work something good out of them?

19. Why do so many marriages—even Christian marriages—end in divorce?

20. What are the consequences of divorce to families, to friends and to society?

What are the consequences of staying in a troubled marriage?

21. How can you help those around you to strengthen their own marriage covenants?

If you have already experienced divorce firsthand, realize that God has not rejected you. Instead, He longs to embrace you, heal the lingering wounds and pour out restoration and blessing over your life—starting right now!

harvesting the fruit

Have you and your spouse stricken the word "divorce" from your vocabulary and made a commitment to unconditional surrender to each other?

22. In what ways has your marriage commitment been tested and made stronger?

In what ways has your marriage commitment been undermined?

23. What do you need to do to strengthen your commitment to your spouse?

Have you developed a secret back door out of your marriage in case the going gets tough? Have you opened that door by entertaining thoughts of calling it quits? If you have, close it right now—nail it shut—through confession and prayer; then commit your marriage to the Lord and receive His grace to continue walking forward in your relationship with your spouse with God as your guide.

Notes

1. Al Janssen, *The Marriage Masterpiece* (Wheaton, IL: Tyndale House Publishers, 2001), p. 67.
2. For more information on marriage covenants, including states that have recently adopted or are considering adoption of legislation, visit http://www.divorcereform.org/cov.html.
3. This is a compilation of several stories. Any resemblance to an actual situation is purely coincidental.

leader's discussion guide

General Guidelines

1. If at all possible, the group should be led by a married couple. This does not mean that both spouses need to be leading the discussions; perhaps one spouse is better at facilitating discussions while the other is better at relationship building or organization—but the leader couple should share responsibilities wherever possible.

2. At the first meeting, be sure to lay down the ground rules for discussions, stressing that following these rules will help everyone feel comfortable during discussion times.

    a. No one should share anything of a personal or potentially embarrassing nature without first asking his or her spouse's permission.

    b. Whatever is discussed in the group meetings is to be held in strictest confidence among group members only.

    c. Allow everyone in the group to participate. However, as a leader, don't force anyone to answer a question if he or she is reluctant. Be sensitive to the different personalities and communication styles among your group members.

3. Fellowship time is very important in building small-group relationships. Providing beverages and/or light refreshments either before or after each session will encourage a time of informal fellowship.

4. Most people live very busy lives; respect the time of your group members by beginning and ending meetings on time.

The Focus on the Family Marriage Ministry Guide *has even more information on starting and leading a small group. You will find this an invaluable resource as you lead others through this Bible study.*

How to Use the Material

1. Each session has more than enough material to cover in a 45-minute teaching period. You will probably not have time to discuss every single question in each session, so prepare for each meeting by selecting questions you feel are most important to address for your group; discuss other questions as time permits. Be sure to save the last 10 minutes of your meeting time for each couple to interact individually and to pray together before adjourning.

    Optional Eight-Session Plan—You can easily divide each session into two parts if you'd like to cover all of the material presented in each session. Each section of the session has enough questions to divide in half, and the Bible study sections (Planting the Seed) are divided into two or three sections that can be taught in separate sessions.

2. Each spouse should have his or her own copy of the book in order to personally answer the questions. The general plan of this study is that the couples complete the questions at home during the week and then bring their books to the meeting to share what they have learned during the week.

    However, the reality of leading small groups in this day and age is that some members will find it difficult to do the homework. If you find that to be the case with your group, consider adjusting the lessons and having members complete the study during your meeting time as you guide them through the lesson. If you use this method, be sure to encourage members to share their individual answers with their spouses during the week (perhaps on a date night).

Session One | The Role Model

A Note to Leaders: This Bible study series is based on The Marriage Masterpiece[1] by Al Janssen. *We highly recommend that you read the prologue and chapters 1 through 5 in preparation for leading this study.*

Before the Meeting

1. Gather materials for making name tags (if couples do not already know each other and/or if you do not already know everyone's name). Also gather extra pens or pencils and Bibles to use as loaners for anyone who needs them.
2. Make photocopies of the Prayer Request Form (see *The Focus on the Family Marriage Ministry Guide*, "Reproducible Forms" section) or provide 3x5-inch index cards for recording requests.
3. Read through your own answers and mark the ones that you especially want to have the group discuss.
4. Prepare slips of paper with the references for the verses that you will want someone to read aloud during the sessions. You can hand out these slips as members arrive, but be sensitive to those who are uncomfortable reading aloud or who might not be familiar with the Bible.

Ice Breakers

1. If this is the first time this couples group has met together, have everyone introduce themselves and tell a little bit about the amount of time they have been married, where they were married, etc.
2. **Option 1**—Invite couples to share a funny thing that happened at their wedding or a how-we-met story.
3. **Option 2**—Have members share their answers to question 6 in Tilling the Ground (p. 13)—about who are their strongest marriage role models.

Discussion

1. **Tilling the Ground**—Begin the discussion by inviting volunteers to share their answers to the questions. (Be sensitive to the time, as you will want to spend most of your discussion time on the next two sections: the Bible study and application sections.)

2. **Planting the Seed**—Lead the group through the Bible study discussion titled "Our Marriage Model" (questions 7 through 17), briefly reviewing the commentary as transitions between the questions. Refrain from reading the commentary word for word, except where necessary for clarity. Save the "Foundational Characteristics of Marriage" (questions 18 through 23) section for the couples to discuss together during the Harvesting the Fruit time.

3. **Watering the Hope**—The questions in this section will help members bring the Bible study into the reality of their own expectations versus God's plan. Don't neglect this part of the study, as it brings the whole lesson into the here and now, applying God's Word to their daily lives.

4. **Harvesting the Fruit**—This section is meant to help the individual couples apply the lesson to their own marriages and can be dealt with in several ways.

   a. Allow the couples one-on-one time at the end of the meeting. This would require space for them to be alone, with enough space between couples to allow for quiet, private conversations.

      If couples have already answered the questions individually, now would be the time to share their answers. Give a time limit, emphasizing that their discussions can be continued at home if they are not able to answer all of the questions in the time allotted.

      If couples have not answered the questions before the meeting, have them answer them together now. This works best when there is open-ended time for the couples to stay until they have completed their discussion and will require that the leaders stay until the last couple has finished.

   b. Instruct couples to complete this section at home during the week after the meeting. This will give them quiet and private time to deal with any issues that might come up and to spend all the time needed to complete the discussion. You will want to follow up at the next meeting to hold couples accountable for completing this part of the lesson.

c. At times it might be advantageous to pair up two couples to discuss these questions. This would help in building accountability into the study.

For this session, encourage each couple to spend time alone sharing their answers to questions 18 through 23 and 28.

5. **Close in Prayer**—An important part of any small-group relationship is the time spent in prayer for one another. This may also be done in a number of ways.

a. Have couples write out their specific prayer requests on the Prayer Request Forms (or index cards). These requests may then be shared with the whole group or traded with another couple as prayer partners for the week. If requests are shared with the whole group, pray as a group before adjourning the meeting; if requests are traded, allow time for the prayer-partner couples to pray together.

b. Gather the whole group together and lead couples in guided prayer, asking that God will continue to open their eyes to His plan for their marriage.

c. Invite each couple to pray individually.

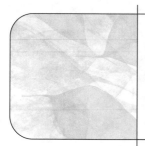

> *Note: Be sensitive to the different levels of spiritual maturity and experiences of the group members. Some may be uncomfortable praying aloud with the whole group or even with their own spouse. Provide a variety of opportunities for different types of prayer experiences from silent prayer to sentence prayers to praying Scripture.*

After the Meeting

1. **Evaluate**—Leaders should spend time evaluating the meeting's effectiveness (see *The Focus on the Family Marriage Ministry Guide*, "Reproducible Forms" section, for an evaluation form).

2. **Encourage**—During the week, try to contact each couple (through phone calls, notes of encouragement or e-mail/instant messaging) and

welcome them to the group. Make yourself available for answering any questions or concerns they may have and generally get to know them. This contact might best be done by the husband-leader contacting the men and the wife-leader contacting the women.

3. **Equip**—Complete the Bible study, even if you have previously gone through this study together.

4. **Pray**—Prayerfully prepare for the next meeting, praying for each couple and for your own preparation.

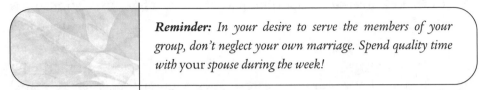

Reminder: In your desire to serve the members of your group, don't neglect your own marriage. Spend quality time with your spouse during the week!

Session Two | The Betrothal

Before the Meeting

1. Gather several Bibles, pens or pencils, and name tags.
2. Make photocopies of the Prayer Request Form or provide 3x5-inch index cards for recording requests.
3. Read through your own answers and mark the ones that you especially want to have the group discuss.
4. Prepare slips of paper with the references for the verses that you will want someone to read aloud during the session. Distribute these slips as members arrive.

Ice Breakers

1. Greet each couple as they arrive.
2. Distribute Prayer Request Forms (or index cards) and ask members to at least write down their name, even if they don't have a specific prayer request. This way, another couple can pray for them during the upcoming week. (After all, just because we don't have a specific request, it doesn't mean we don't need prayer!)
3. Invite volunteers to share how they applied what they learned in last week's session. Here are some suggested questions to ask:
    a. How did you see your spouse model a godly attribute during the past week?
    b. What is one thing that you learned in last week's meeting that helped you understand (or illustrate) God's model?
4. **Option**—Invite couples to share their funny or touching engagement stories.

Discussion

1. **Tilling the Ground**—Explain that you want to take a poll about engagement lengths. Ask everyone to stand up and then respond to the following:

a. If you were engaged less than six months before your wedding, sit down.

b. If you were engaged less than one year, sit down.

c. Less than two years, sit down.

d. Continue until everyone is sitting down. Then discuss questions 4 and 5.

2. **Planting the Seed**—Discuss questions 6 through 18.

3. **Watering the Hope**—Have each couple pair up with another couple to discuss this section.

a. Give the couples several minutes to discuss their answers. If time is short, have them discuss questions 24 through 26 only.

b. Have couples share with the whole group their answers to question 26.

4. **Harvesting the Fruit**—Have spouses pair up and share their answers to questions 27 and 28. Instruct couples to make a date to reenact their marriage proposal or to at least have a romantic dinner to reminisce about that special time.

5. **Close in Prayer**—Have couples pray together following the direction at the end of the session. As couples leave, have members each select someone else's Prayer Request Form (or index card) so that they can pray for that person during the coming week.

After the Meeting

1. **Evaluate.**

2. **Encourage**—Call each couple and ask if they have reenacted their marriage proposal or at least shared memories of that special day. Invite couples to bring a favorite wedding photo or to prepare to share a touching or funny incident from their wedding.

3. **Equip.**

4. **Pray** that each couple would use their time this week to enjoy the memory of their engagement.

Session Three | The Ceremony

Before the Meeting

1. Gather index cards, pens or pencils, and Bibles, as needed.
2. Make photocopies of the Prayer Request Form or provide 3x5-inch index cards for recording requests.
3. Read through your own answers and mark the ones that you especially want to have the group discuss.
4. Prepare slips of paper with the references for the verses that you will want someone to read aloud during the session. Distribute these slips as members arrive.
5. Set up a place for members to display their wedding photos. You could use available bulletin-board or wall space, or provide poster board on which you could tape the photos. Be careful not to damage photos with either tacks or tape.

Ice Breakers

1. Distribute Prayer Request Forms (or index cards) to members as they arrive.
2. Instruct them to display their wedding photos.
3. Invite couples to share about their photo or about a funny or touching incident from their weddings.

Discussion

1. **Tilling the Ground**—Discuss questions 1 through 6 (answers to question 5 may have been covered during the ice breaker).
2. **Planting the Seed**—Discuss questions 7 through 19 as time allows. Questions 20 through 27 may be discussed by individual couples during the Harvesting the Fruit time.
3. **Watering the Hope**—Discuss questions 28 through 30.

4. **Harvesting the Fruit**—Have spouses share with each other their answers to questions 20 through 27, 31 and 32.

5. **Close in Prayer**—Have each couple partner with another to share what each has written on his or her Prayer Request Form (or index card). Once they've shared, encourage the paired couples to pray together.

After the Meeting

1. **Evaluate.**

2. **Encourage** the prayer-partner couples to contact one another during the week to share answers to prayer. For the next meeting, ask couples to find at least one example of how our world seems to encourage lack of commitment. These might be in the form of magazine or newspaper ads, or videotaped clips of movies, TV shows or advertisements. If it is not possible to share these visuals, instruct members to look for examples throughout the week and be prepared to share what they've observed.

3. **Equip.**

4. **Pray** that couples will demonstrate their recommitment in tangible ways.

Session Four | The Commitment

Before the Meeting

1. Provide pens or pencils and Bibles, as needed.
2. Make photocopies of the Study Review Form (see *The Focus on the Family Marriage Ministry Guide*, "Reproducible Forms" section).
3. Make photocopies of the Prayer Request For or provide 3x5-inch index cards for recording requests.
4. Read through your own answers and mark the ones that you especially want to have the group discuss.
5. Prepare slips of paper with the references for the verses that you will want someone to read aloud during the session. (You can distribute these slips as members arrive.)
6. During the week, collect samples of how our world seems to encourage lack of commitment, or encourage group members to bring samples to the meeting. This might be in the form of magazine or newspaper ads, or videotaped clips of movies, TV shows or advertisements. If it is not possible to share these visuals, instruct members to look for examples throughout the week and be prepared to share what they've observed.

> **Note:** *Be sensitive to the members of your group who may have been divorced and may be in a second (or third) marriage. Assure them that God loves them and that whatever mistakes they may have made in the past, He will forgive and heal past hurts.*

Ice Breakers

1. Invite members to complete their Prayer Request Forms.
2. Share the examples of lack of commitment from the media or society at large.

Discussion

1. **Tilling the Ground**—Discuss question 3.
2. **Planting the Seed**—Discuss questions 4 through 16 as time permits.
3. **Watering the Hope**—Read the story, and lead discussion of the questions that follow.
4. **Harvesting the Fruit**—Have individual couples share their answers privately.
5. **Close in Prayer**—Ask group members to stand in a circle, and allow time for sentence prayers of praise and worship. Close by singing a worship song together.

After the Meeting

1. **Evaluate**—Distribute the Study Review Forms for members to take home with them. Share the importance of feedback, and ask members to take the time this week to write their review of the group meetings and then to return them to you.
2. **Encourage**—Call each couple during the next week and invite them to join you for the next study in the *Focus on the Family Marriage Series*.

Note
1. Al Janssen, *The Marriage Masterpiece* (Wheaton, IL: Tyndale House Publishers, 2001).

Welcome to the Family!

As you participate in the *Focus on the Family Marriage Series*, it is our prayerful hope that God will deepen your understanding of His plan for marriage and that He will strengthen your marriage relationship.

This series is just one of the many helpful, insightful, and encouraging resources produced by Focus on the Family. In fact, that's what Focus on the Family is all about—providing inspiration, information, and biblically based advice to people in all stages of life.

It began in 1977 with the vision of one man, Dr. James Dobson, a licensed psychologist and author of 18 best-selling books on marriage, parenting, and family. Alarmed by the societal, political, and economic pressures that were threatening the existence of the American family, Dr. Dobson founded Focus on the Family with one employee and a once-a-week radio broadcast aired on only 36 stations.

Now an international organization, the ministry is dedicated to preserving Judeo-Christian values and strengthening and encouraging families through the life-changing message of Jesus Christ. Focus ministries reach families worldwide through 10 separate radio broadcasts, two television news features, 13 publications, 18 Web sites, and a steady series of books and award-winning films and videos for people of all ages and interests.

We'd love to hear from you!

For more information about the ministry, or if we can be of help to your family, simply write to Focus on the Family, Colorado Springs, CO 80995 or call 1-800-A-FAMILY (1-800-232-6459). Friends in Canada may write Focus on the Family, P.O. Box 9800, Stn. Terminal, Vancouver, B.C. V6B 4G3 or call 1-800-661-9800. Visit our Web site—www.family.org—to learn more about Focus on the Family or to find out if there is an associate office in your country.

Strengthen and enrich your marriage with these Focus on the Family® relationship builders.

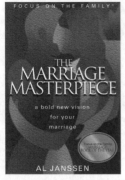

The Marriage Masterpiece

Now that you've discovered the richness to be had in "The Focus on the Family Marriage Series" Bible studies, be sure to read the book the series is based on. *The Marriage Masterpiece* takes a fresh appraisal of the exquisite design God has for a man and woman. Explaining the reasons why this union is meant to last a lifetime, it also shows how God's relationship with humanity is the model for marriage. Rediscover the beauty and worth of marriage in a new light with this thoughtful, creative book. A helpful study guide is included for group discussion. Hardcover.

The Love List

Marriage experts Drs. Les and Leslie Parrot present eight healthy habits that refresh, transform and restore the intimacy of your marriage relationship. Filled with practical suggestions, this book will help you make daily, weekly, monthly and yearly improvements in your marriage. Hardcover.

Capture His Heart/Capture Her Heart

Lysa TerKeurst has written two practical guides—one for wives and one for husbands—that will open your eyes to the needs, desires and longings of your spouse. These two books each offer eight essential criteria plus creative tips for winning and holding his or her heart. Paperback set.

• • •

Look for these special books in your Christian bookstore or request a copy by calling 1-800-A-FAMILY (1-800-232-6459). Friends in Canada may write Focus on the Family, P.O. Box 9800, Stn. Terminal, Vancouver, B.C. V6B 4G3 or call 1-800-661-9800.

Visit our Web site (www.family.org) to learn more about the ministry or find out if there is a Focus on the Family office in your country.

STRENGTHEN MARRIAGES.
STRENGTHEN YOUR CHURCH.

Here's Everything You Need for a Dynamic Marriage Ministry!

Focus on the Family ® Marriage Series Group Starter Kit
Kit Box • Bible Study/Marriage • ISBN 08307.32365

Group Starter Kit includes:

- Seven Bible Studies: *The Masterpiece Marriage, The Passionate Marriage, The Fighting Marriage, The Model Marriage, The Surprising Marriage, The Giving Marriage* and *The Covenant Marriage*

- *The Focus on the Family Marriage Ministry Guide*

- *An Introduction to the Focus on the Family Marriage Series* video

Pick up the *Focus on the Family Marriage Series* where Christian books are sold.

Gospel Light

Devotionals for Drawing Near to God and One Another

Moments Together for Couples
Hardcover • 384p
ISBN 08307.17544

Moments Together for Parents
Gift Hardcover
96p
ISBN 08307.32497

Moments Together for Intimacy
Gift Hardcover
96p
ISBN 08307.32489

Give Your Marriage a Checkup

The Marriage Checkup
How Healthy
Is Your Marriage Really?
Paperback • 140p
ISBN 08307.30699

The Marriage Checkup Questionnaire
An Easy-to-Use Questionnaire
to Help You Evaluate the
Health of Your Marriage
Manual • 24p
ISBN 08307.30648

How to Counsel a Couple in 6 Sessions or Less
A Tool for Marriage Counseling
to Use in Tandem with the
Marriage Checkup Questionnaire
Manual • 24p
ISBN 08307.30680

Complete Your Marriage-Strengthening Library

Preparing for Marriage
The Complete Guide
to Help You Discover God's Plan
for a Lifetime of Love
Dennis Rainey
Paperback • 170p
ISBN 08307.17803
Counselor's Pack
(3 books, I Leader's Guide)
ISBN 08307.21568
Couples Pack (2 books) • ISBN 08307.21576
Leader's Guide • ISBN 08307.17609

Communication: Key to Your Marriage
A Practical Guide to Creating
a Happy, Fulfilling Relationship
Dr. H. Norman Wright
Paperback • 244p
ISBN 08307.25334
Video Approx. 2 hrs.
UPC 607135.004639

Holding on to Romance
Keeping Your Marriage
Alive and Passionate
After the Honeymoon Years
Dr. H. Norman Wright
Video • Approx. 1 hr.
UPC 85116.00779

Gospel Light